ART & DESIGN CAREERS

# A Career in ANIMATION

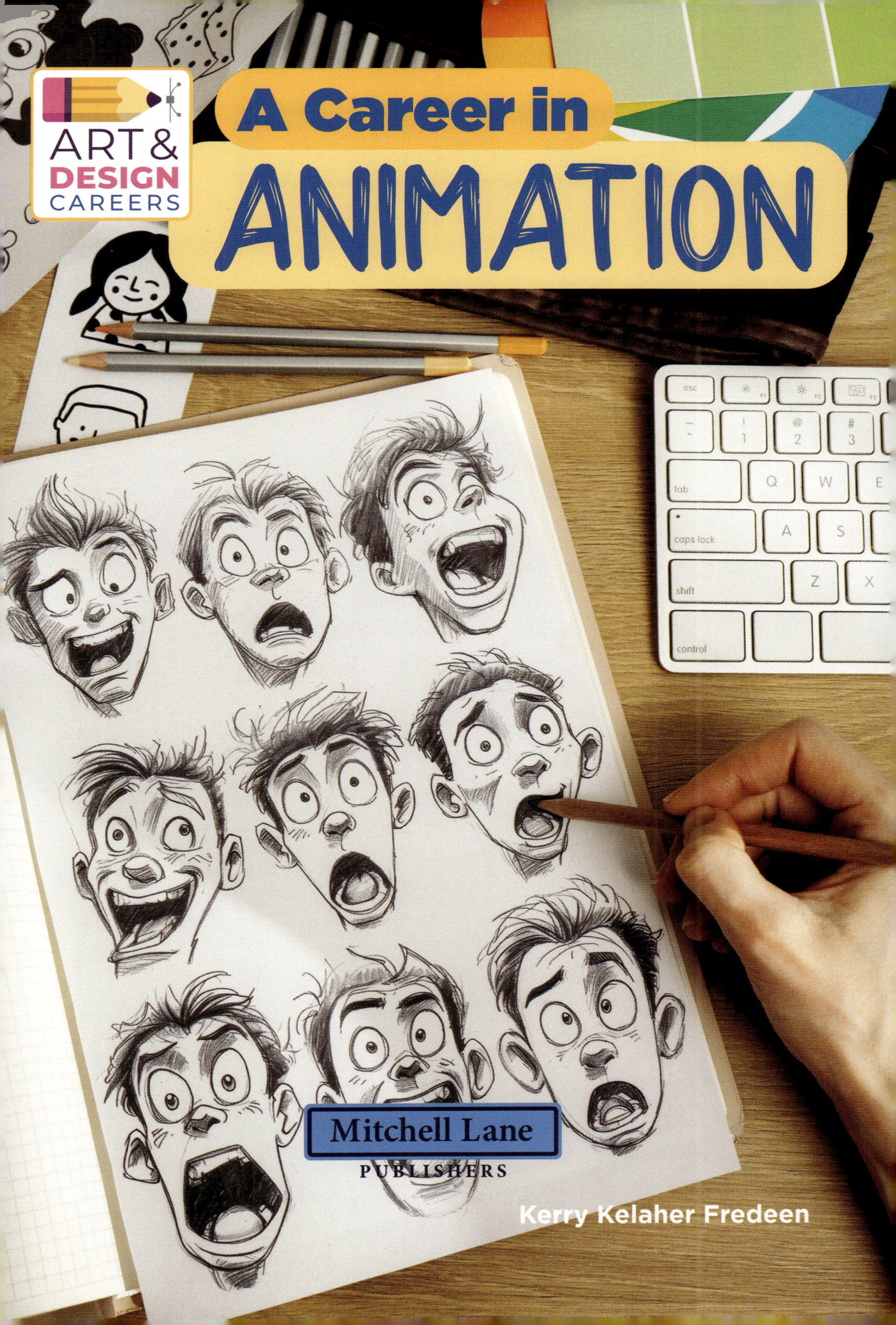

Mitchell Lane PUBLISHERS

Kerry Kelaher Fredeen

Mitchell Lane
PUBLISHERS

mitchelllanepub.com

2001 SW 31st Avenue
Hallandale, FL 33009



First Edition, 2026.
Author: Kerry Kelaher Fredeen
Designer: Ed Morgan
Editor: Tammy Gagne

Series: Art and Design Careers
Title: A Career in Animation

Library bound ISBN: 979-8-89260-498-7
eBook ISBN: 979-8-89260-513-7

Photo credits: cover, contents, p. 5, 21, 23, 27, 29, 39, 41, 43 freepik.com; p. 7, 9, 13, 15, 17, 19, 25, 31, 33, 35, 37 Alamy; p. 11 wikimedia

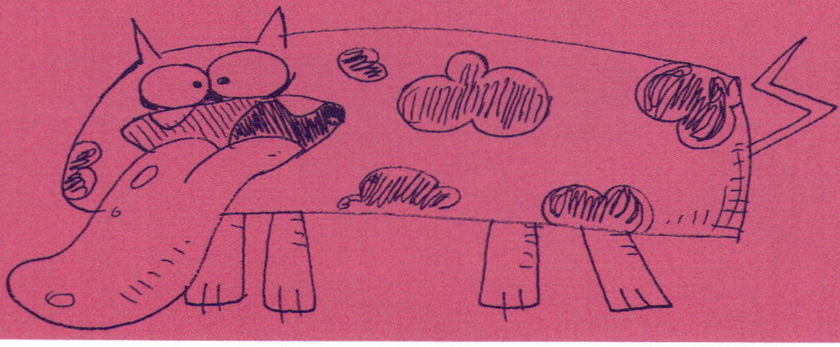

# Contents



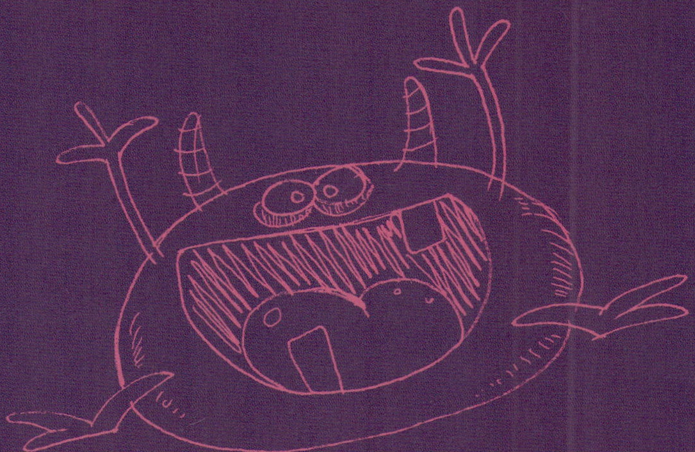

# Chapter One

# Art in Motion

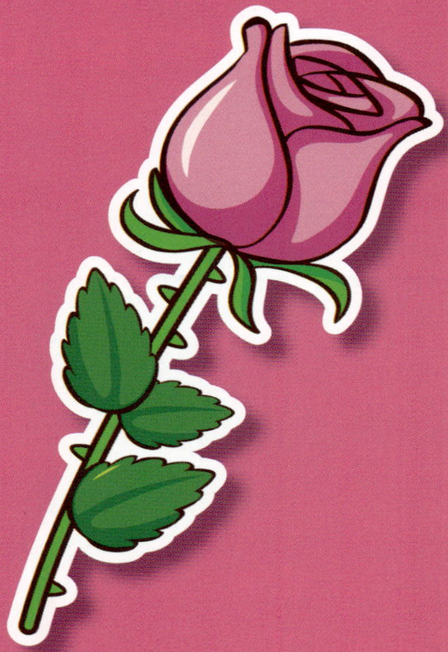

Mechele was confident in her style. From the unusual spelling of her name to her artistic talent, she had always been glad that she stood out in a crowd. She had been working on her project for the school art fair for months. Other students had submitted traditional artwork. There were paintings, drawings, and photographs. There were even some sculptures. But Mechele's project was unique.

Mechele had created a flipbook. Forty pages long, it was entirely hand drawn and water colored. Each page featured a single pink rose. The first picture showed a tiny rosebud, but as one flipped through the book, the rose began opening until the glorious flower was in full bloom.

# CHAPTER ONE

The project wasn't easy. Each page had to be just slightly different from the page before it. These gradual changes gave the book its **animated** effect. Mechele spent hours on each page, making sure the images blended smoothly. She also wanted the rose to look as lifelike as possible.

Mechele was a fan of old-fashioned animation. She especially liked the early, hand-drawn films of Walt Disney. She tried to give her flipbook a similar look and feel to those classic movies she cherished.

The judges were moving from artist to artist, carefully considering everyone's work. Mechele held her breath as Ms. Santos, the art teacher, approached her project. The teacher picked up the book and looked through it.

"I love your flipbook, Mechele. These drawings are lovely," Ms. Santos said. "And the **consistency** is impressive. This must have taken you a lot of time."

# Art in Motion

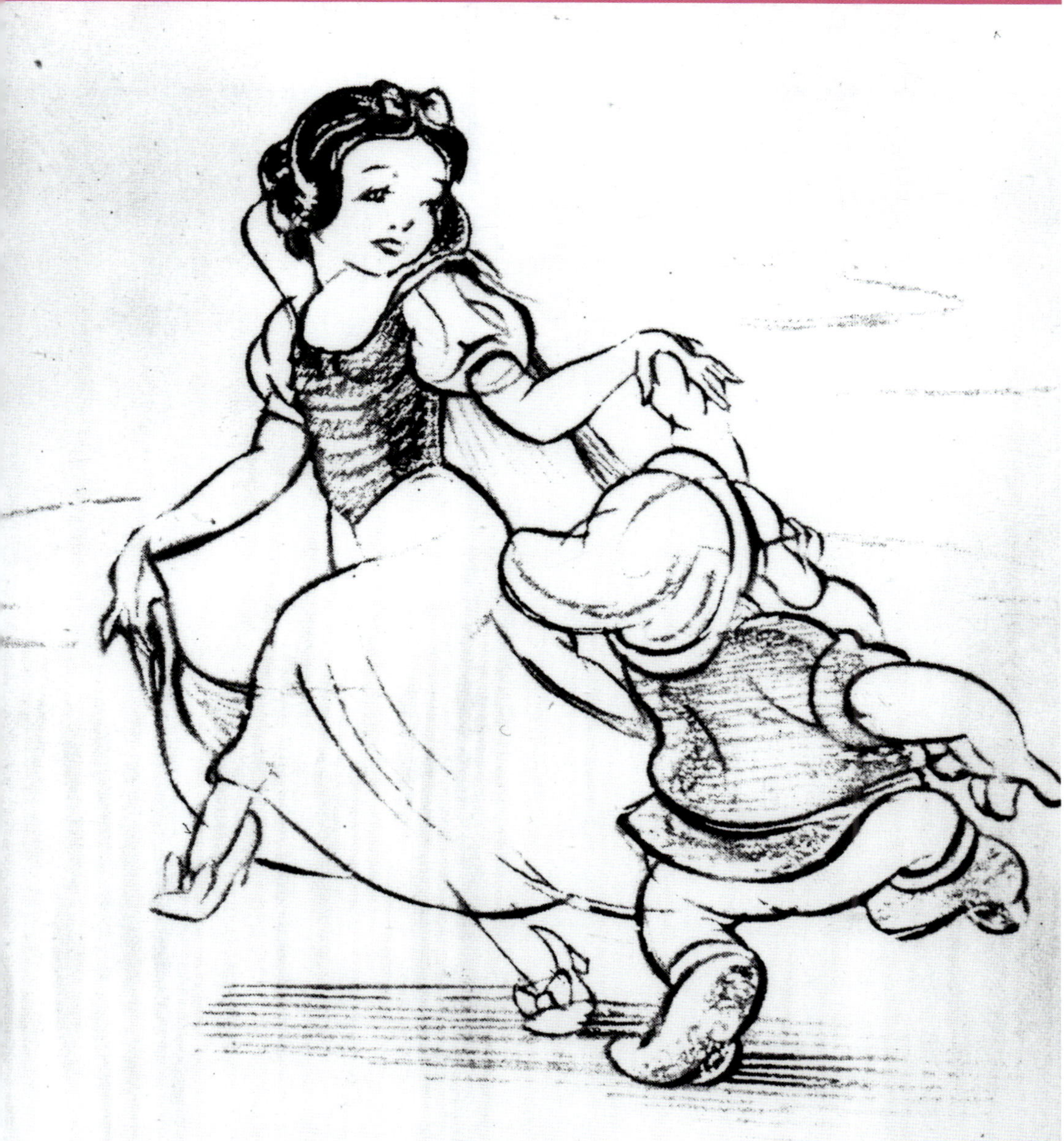

An early sketch from Disney's animated classic
*Snow White and the Seven Dwarfs*.

## CHAPTER ONE

"It did," Mechele replied. "I spent several hours on each page. I wanted to get everything just right. I knew it would require a lot of work, but I enjoyed every minute of it. I have always loved animation. In fact, I'm hoping to get a job working in the field one day."

"I think that could be a great career for you," Ms. Santos said. "Have you thought about your next steps? I know of some animation camps you might be interested in. And the school art club is always looking for new members."

"I never thought about an animation camp. I'd love to find out more," Mechele told the teacher. "I'm already looking into colleges that offer animation courses for when I graduate. I'd love to get an **internship** at one of the studios. I'm exploring all my options."

"I think you have a great shot," Ms. Santos said, "at both an internship and scoring a prize in this art competition."

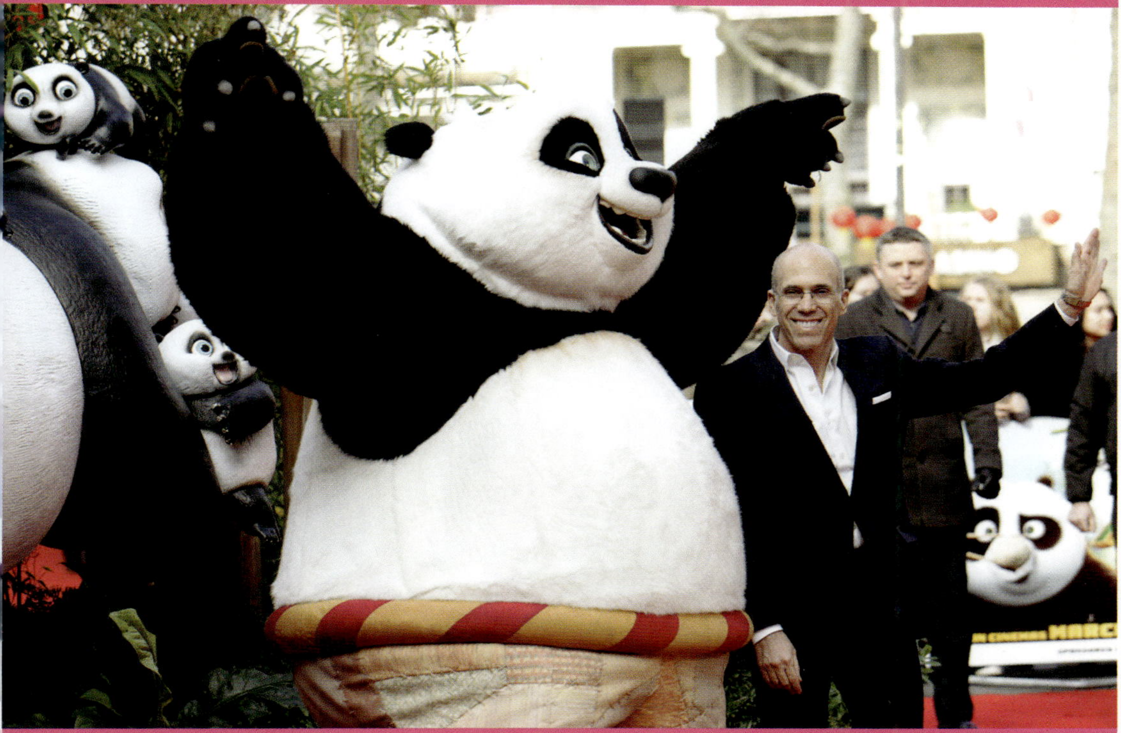

# A Winning Team

**Being an animator often means being part of a team. Some animated films have more than one hundred animators working together to bring the project to life. Jeffrey Katzenberg is among the founders of DreamWorks Studios. In an interview with Google, he said, "It is a team sport. . . . [I]t really takes a village of people, of artists, with a shared vision."**

# Chapter Two

# Animation's Beginnings

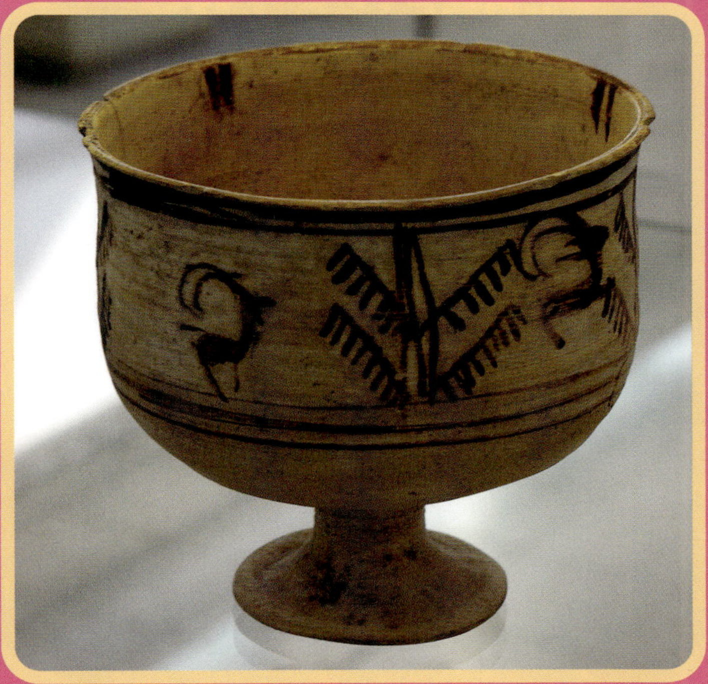

This ancient bowl is one of the earliest examples of animation.

Animation is the art of making still objects appear to move. When most people think of animation, they think of cartoons, movies, or video games. But animation existed long before these modern forms of entertainment. One of the earliest examples is a piece of pottery from 5000 BCE. Five images of a goat were painted on this bowl, which was found in Iran in the 1970s. When a person spins the bowl, the goat appears to leap.

# CHAPTER TWO

Another early animation machine was called the zoetrope. This spinning drum had pictures inside that appeared to move. People could replace the strips of pictures inside the zoetrope, so they could see new images when they used it again. But with the zoetrope, only one person could view the animation at a time.

A new device moved past that limitation in 1892. Charles-Émile Reynaud, a French inventor, came up with a way to project animated images onto a screen. Called the Optical Theatre, his device could show an animated movie to a crowd. Reynaud's invention set animation on a new path.

# Animation's Beginnings

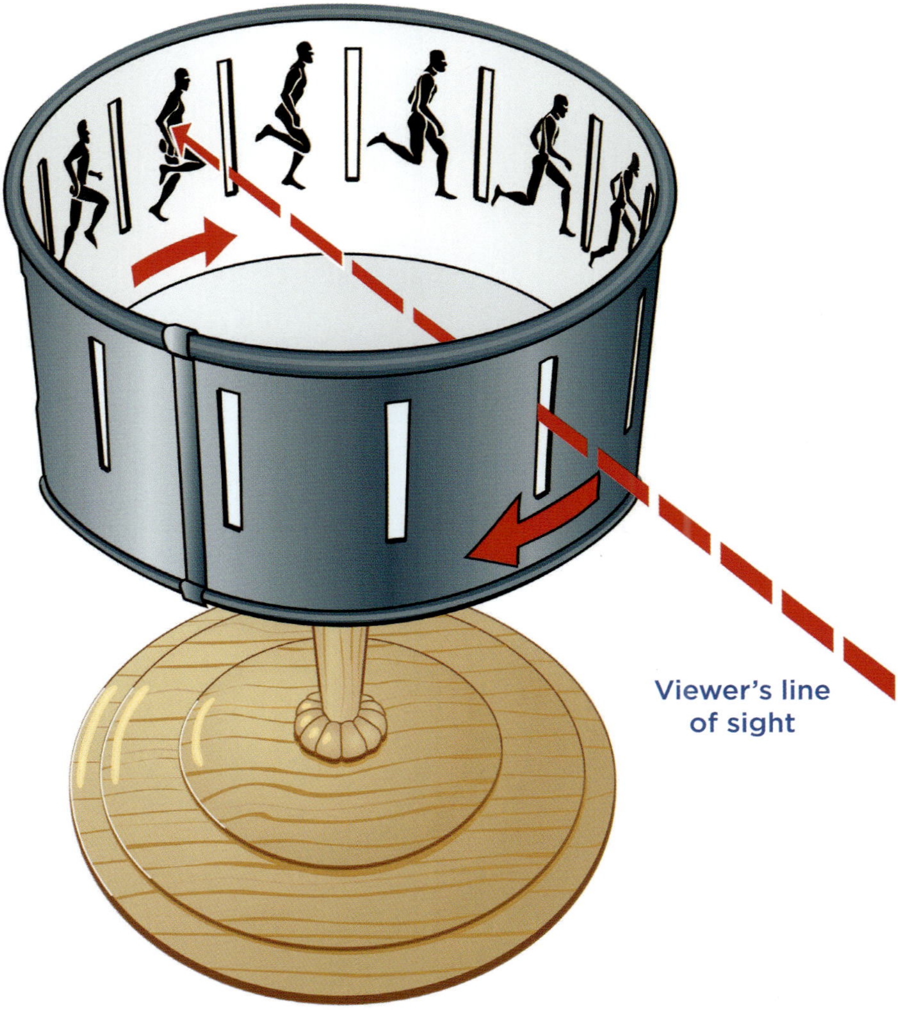


The zoetrope was an early form of animation technology.

# CHAPTER TWO

In 1919, a young man named Walt Disney was working at an art studio in Kansas City, Missouri. Disney worked mostly on commercials. Then he met cartoonist Ub Iwerks, and the pair decided to start their own animation studio. After a few years in Kansas City without much success, they moved to Hollywood in 1923 and started Walt Disney Studios. They created a character called Oswald the Lucky Rabbit, which they later turned into Mickey Mouse. In 1938, the studio released its first full-length film, *Snow White and the Seven Dwarfs*. The film was a hit, and Disney won an honorary Academy Award. The studio created many more animated films in the coming decades.

# Animation's Beginnings

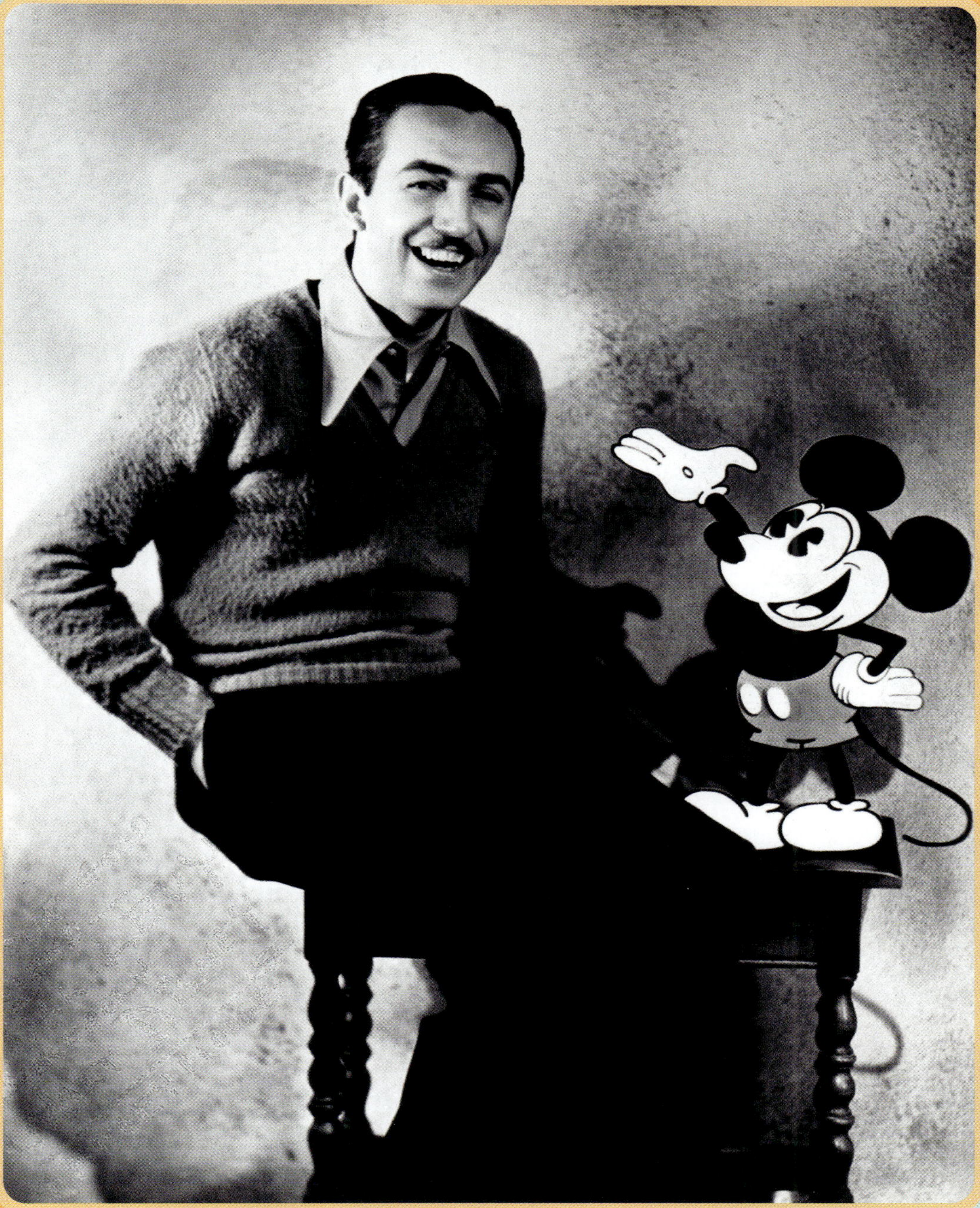

Walt Disney and his creation Mickey Mouse

# CHAPTER TWO

Although Walt Disney died in 1966, his legacy in animation remains through his still successful company. The 1991 Disney film *Beauty and the Beast* was the first animated movie to be **nominated** for an Oscar, another name for an Academy Award, in the Best Picture category.

Disney wasn't the only one producing animation in the early 1900s. On the other side of the world, Japanese anime was born. These hand-drawn animations became enormously popular, but a terrible earthquake in 1923 destroyed the artwork of many anime studios. The industry eventually worked its way back. Today, it is more popular than ever.

# Animation's Beginnings

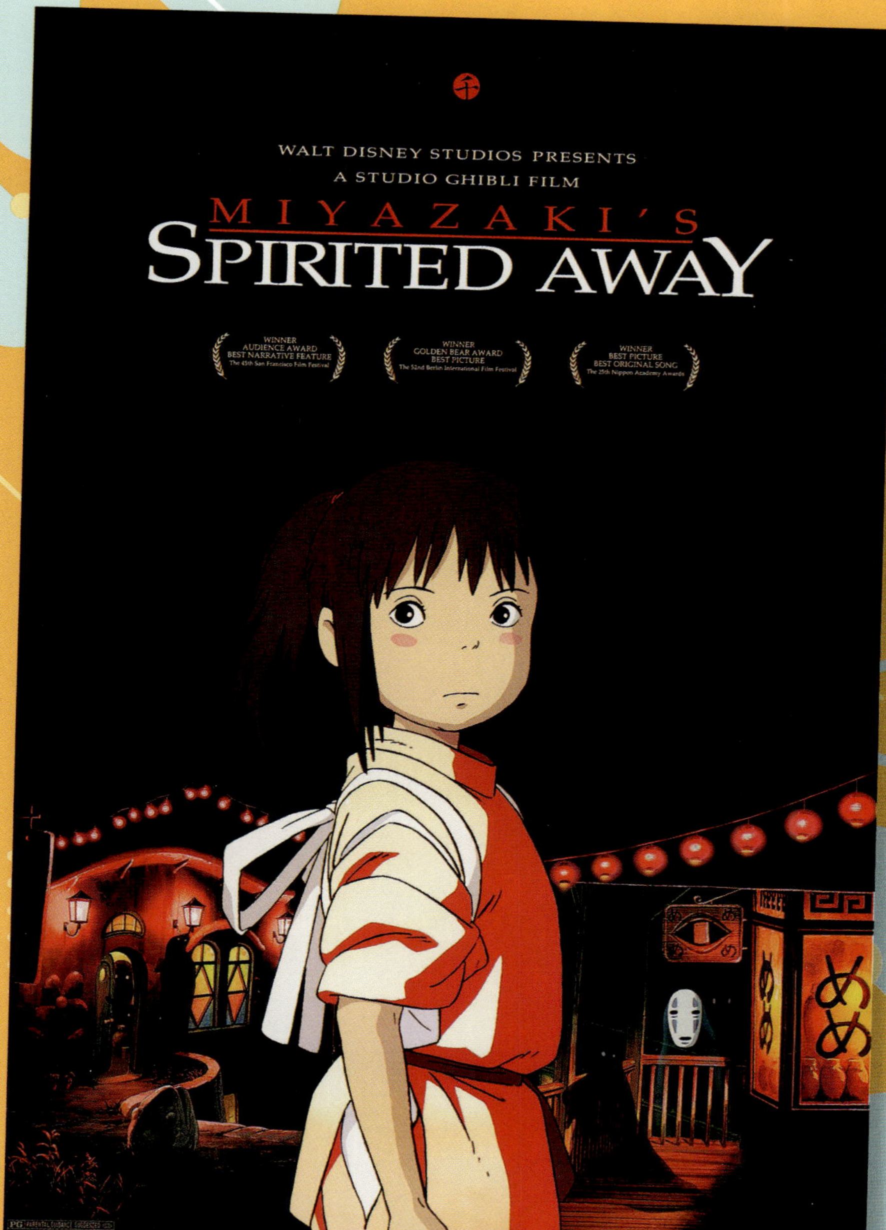


The Japanese anime film *Spirited Away* won the Academy Award for Best Animated Feature in 2003.

# CHAPTER TWO

Animation isn't just shown in theaters, though. *The Flintstones* ran in a prime-time television slot from 1960 to 1966. This animated series was set in prehistoric times and was created for both kids and adults. Beginning in the 1960s, Saturday morning cartoons were also popular. Millions of kids spent every Saturday morning watching *Scooby-Doo*, *Bugs Bunny*, and *The Smurfs* over the next several decades.

In 1989, animation came back to prime-time TV with *The Simpsons*. Animator Matt Groening had been making short, animated cartoons for *The Tracey Ullman Show*, and their popularity led to a new series based on the characters. As of 2024, *The Simpsons* was the longest running animated series in TV history. Groening told *USA Today*, "The show is such a part of the pop culture landscape that whole different generations have discovered it."

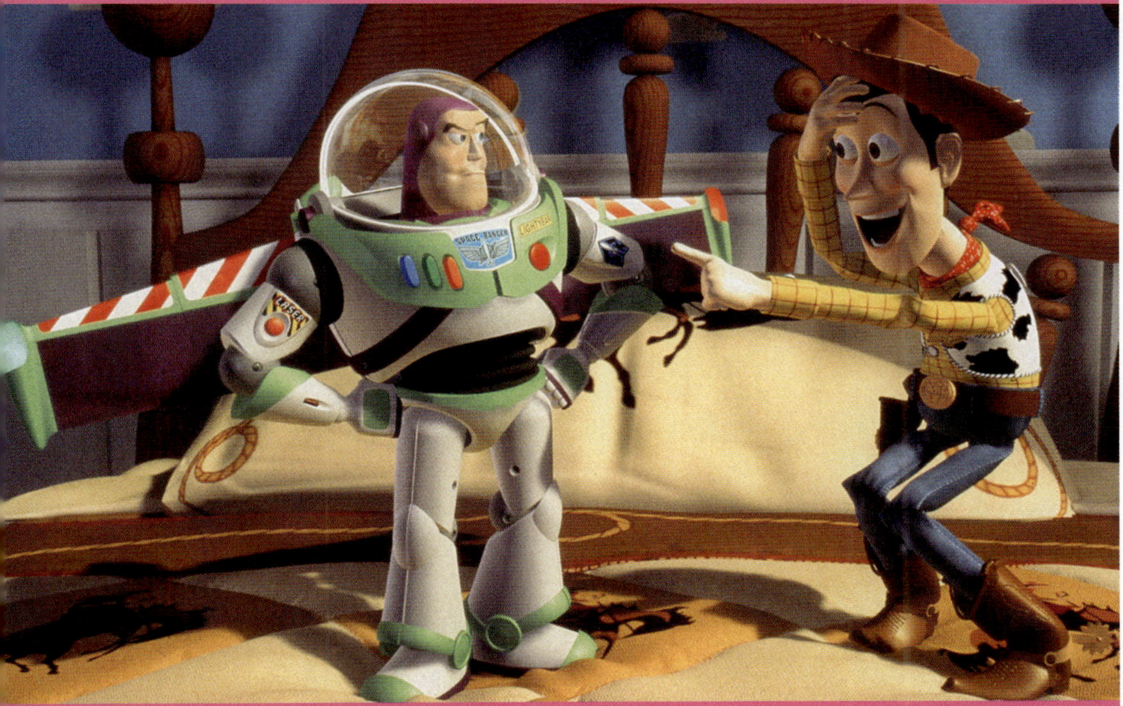

# Pixar Animation Studios

The computer animation company Pixar was launched in 1986. In the beginning, the company made short films and TV commercials. But in 1995, Pixar released the first fully computer animated feature film, *Toy Story*. Since then, Pixar movies have won numerous Academy Awards. Many of the company's films have also been big hits at the box office.

# Chapter Three

# Animation Skills and Tools

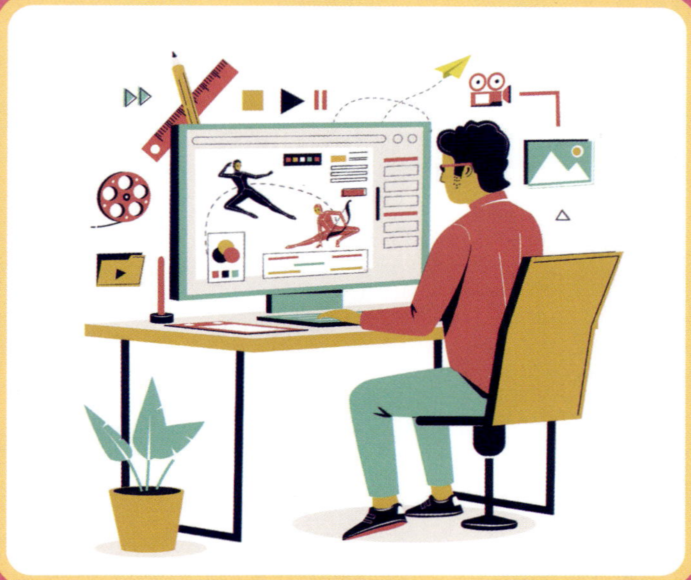

Animators are artists. A successful animator needs highly developed drawing skills. An animator must also have a clear understanding of how the human body moves. Angela Lepito, an artist manager at DreamWorks Animation, shares that animators use this knowledge to shape their characters' movements. As Lepito explains in an article on the *Oxford Academic* website, "Animators push and pull, squash, and stretch beyond real-world boundaries to bring forth the illusion of life."

# CHAPTER THREE

Animators are also storytellers. They use visual elements to build emotion and connection to their characters. Animators use storyboards to organize their projects. A storyboard is a series of drawings that show the plot and action of a film.

There are many styles of animation. Traditional animation, also known as cel animation, is hand drawn on **transparent** plastic. Each frame of the film is separately drawn and photographed. This process was used in many of the animated films of the twentieth century. It is costly and takes a long time, but it is still used by some animation companies.

When computers became more advanced in the 1970s, computer animation began. Computer generated imagery (CGI) was used in the 1977 live action film *Star Wars*. Two-dimensional, or 2D, computer animation became common in film, TV, and video games during the 1980s. By the 1990s, three-dimensional, or 3D, computer animation was becoming popular. The TV show *Veggie Tales* became the first fully 3D animated series in the United States in 1993.

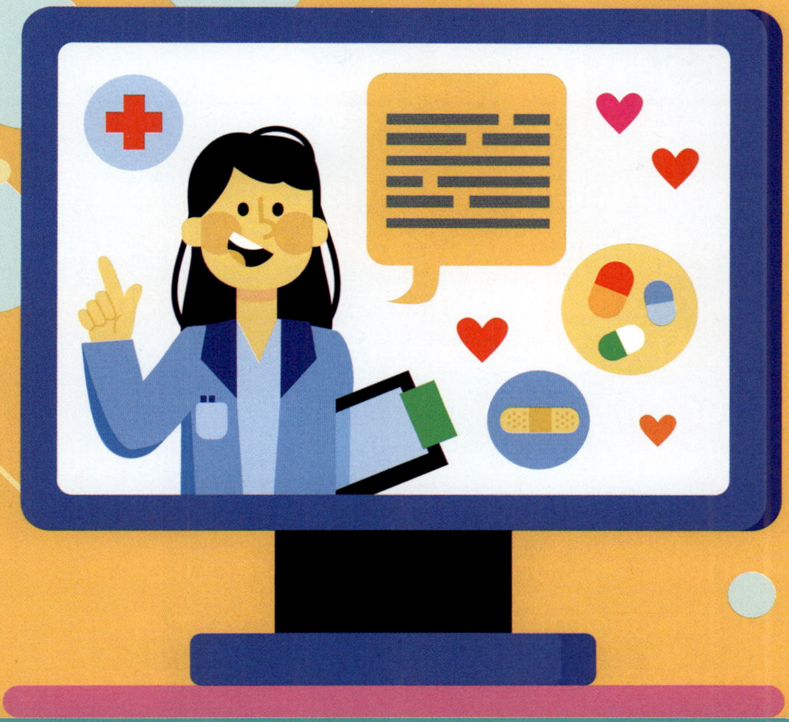

# Careers Outside Entertainment

Many people think that animation is just for movies, TV, and video games. But there are also jobs for animators outside those fields. Medical animators build instructional films as training tools for doctors and patients. And **forensic** animators help police solve cases by recreating accidents and crime scenes.

# CHAPTER THREE

In stop motion animation, an object is photographed, then moved slightly and photographed again. The **succession** of frames gives the appearance of motion. Tim Burton's 1993 film *The Nightmare Before Christmas* was created using stop motion animation.

Motion capture animation records an actor's movements. These movements are then sent to a computer. The actor wears a special suit with sensors that capture the person's movements and facial expressions. The animator can use this data to create a realistic animated character. Motion capture was used to turn actor Andy Serkis into Gollum in the *Lord of the Rings* movie series.

# Animation Skills and Tools

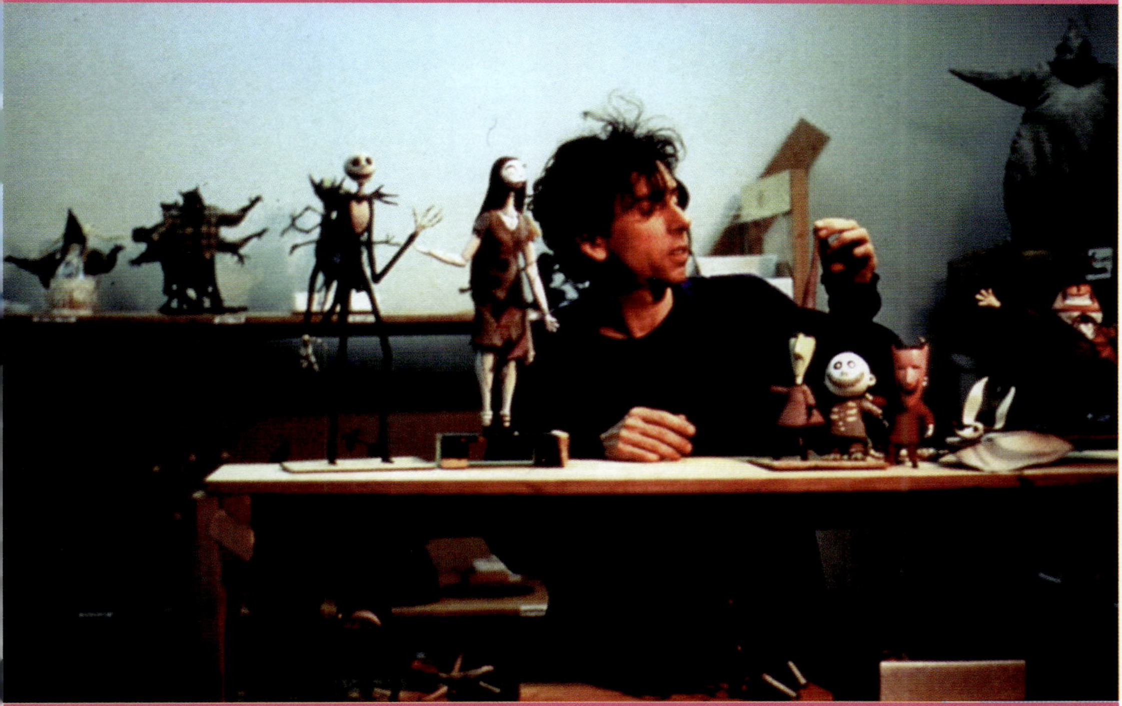

Director and animator Tim Burton at work on 1993's *The Nightmare Before Christmas*.

# CHAPTER THREE

Each type of animation requires different skills. But there are some traits every animator must possess. First, an animator must be creative with great attention to detail. A person in this career must also be able to set priorities and meet deadlines. Animation projects take a long time, so an animator also needs patience. Since most animators work in teams, communication skills are essential.

Many animation jobs require a college degree. Both two- and four-year animation programs are offered at many colleges and universities. To prepare for college, a budding animator can take art and drawing classes in high school. Computer and science courses are also helpful. Joining an art or film club or drawing comics for the school paper can be a great way to gain experience for this career.

# Animation Skills and Tools

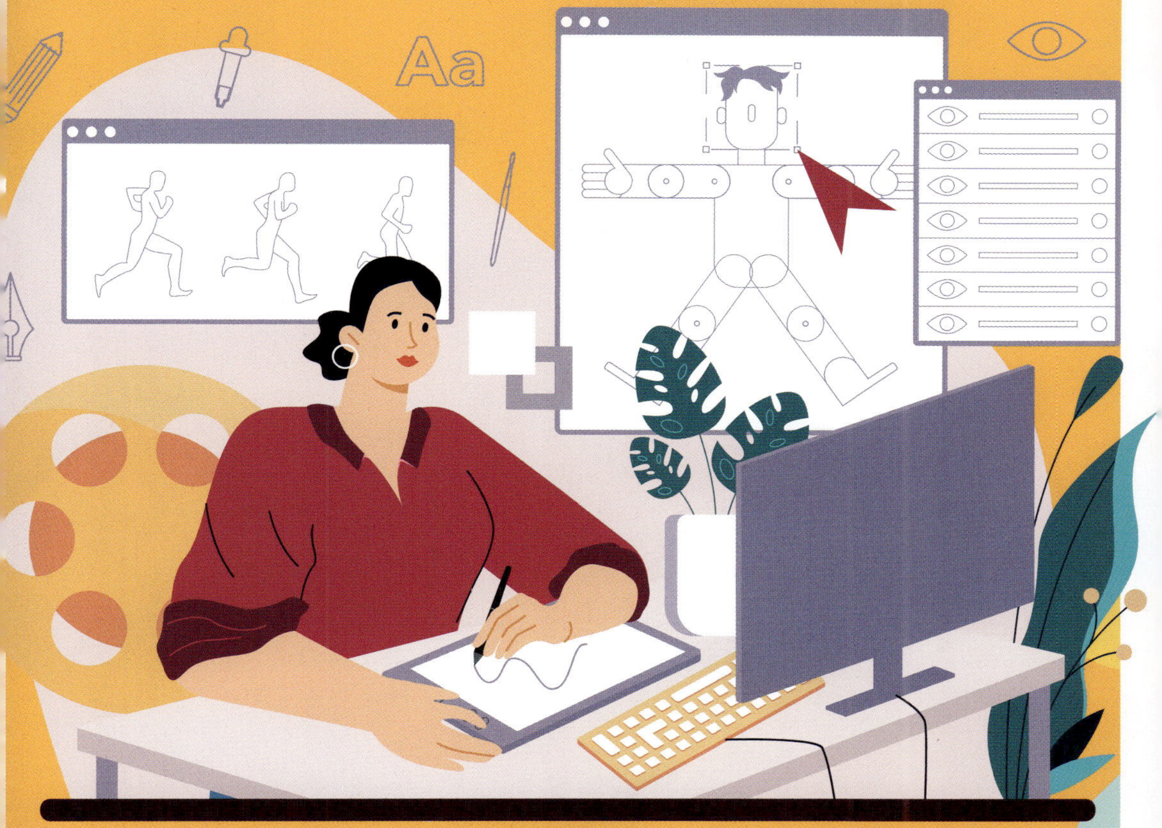


Animators use a lot of tools to get the job done.

## Chapter Four

# The Many Tasks of Animation

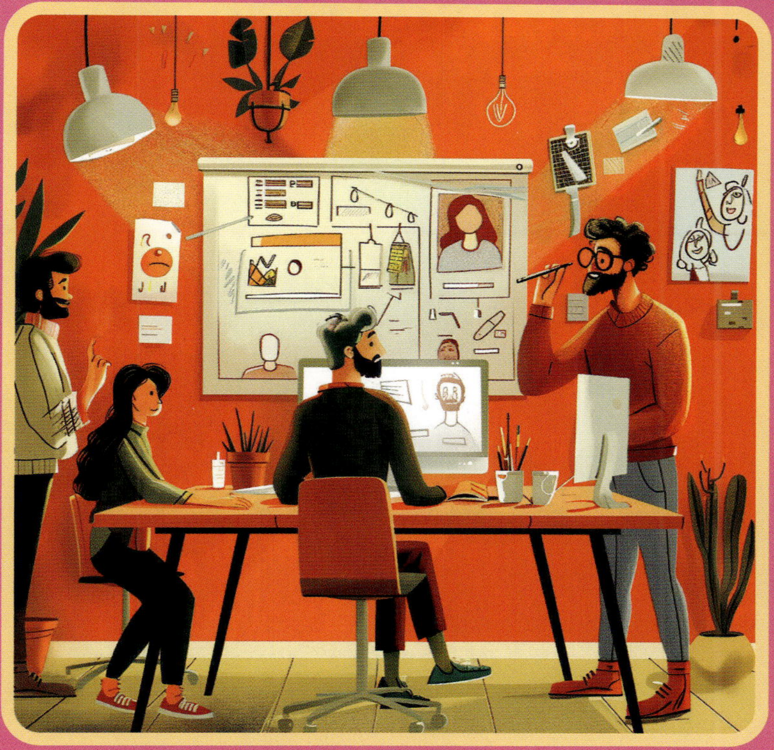

Some people assume that an animator sits at a desk drawing all day. Drawing, whether by hand or on a computer, is indeed a big part of this job. But there are many other important tasks that animators must perform.

Animators attend many meetings with the rest of their team to discuss projects. They also spend time showing their work to supervisors and directors. This helps keep their work in line with the creative vision for the project.

# CHAPTER FOUR

Most animators work in an animation studio. Working around other animators gives them a chance to share ideas. Some animators work from home offices part of the time, attending meetings as needed.

Sometimes animators travel for research. Pixar animators visited Oaxaca, Mexico, before creating the 2017 film *Coco*. The film's codirector, Adrian Molina, thought the animators should observe Mexican culture. "We knew it was very important to do the research, to get every detail recorded, so that when we get back to Pixar . . . it can all come from an informed place," Molina told the *Disney News* website.

Most animation projects start with a script and a storyboard. An animator will create a storyboard based on a writer's script for the project. For smaller projects, the animator might double as the scriptwriter.

# The Many Tasks of Animation

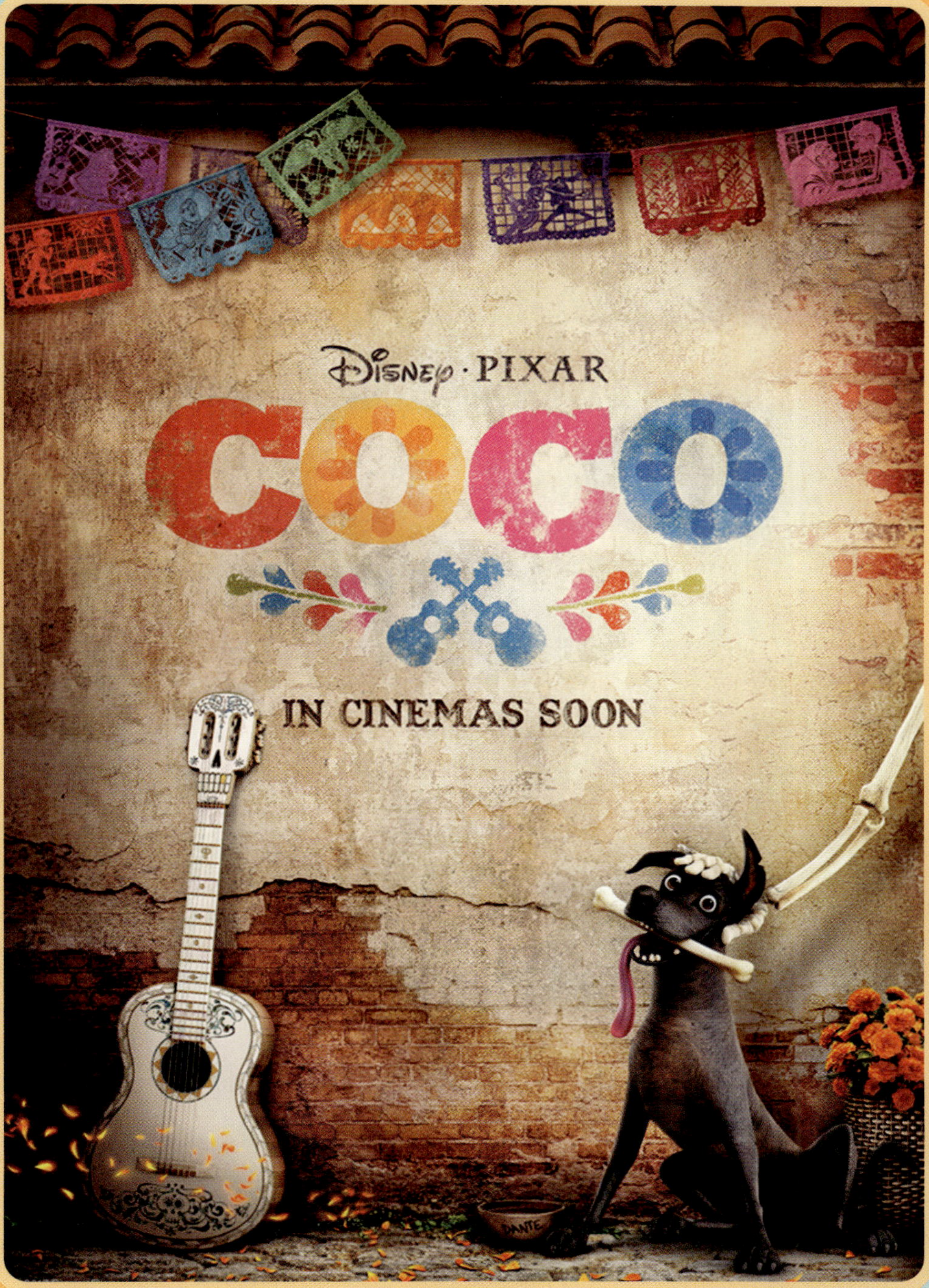


The animators of *Coco* visited Mexico to observe its culture.

# CHAPTER FOUR

Animators refer to the storyboard as they begin drawing characters and scenes. To help with this process, some animators set up props to look at while drawing. These are known as assets.

After the animation is completed, the animator needs to add lighting. This works similarly to lighting in photography. Lighting adds depth and detail to the animation. It also helps create a mood.

Once this step is finished, it's time for rendering. This is a process that takes all the elements and effects that have been created and combines them. The animation is run through a computer program that creates the final shots.

With everything in place, it's time for compositing. This step takes rendered images and other elements, such as graphics and text, and combines them into a sequence. Compositing brings the project together and prepares it for editing, the final stage in the production process.

# The Many Tasks of Animation

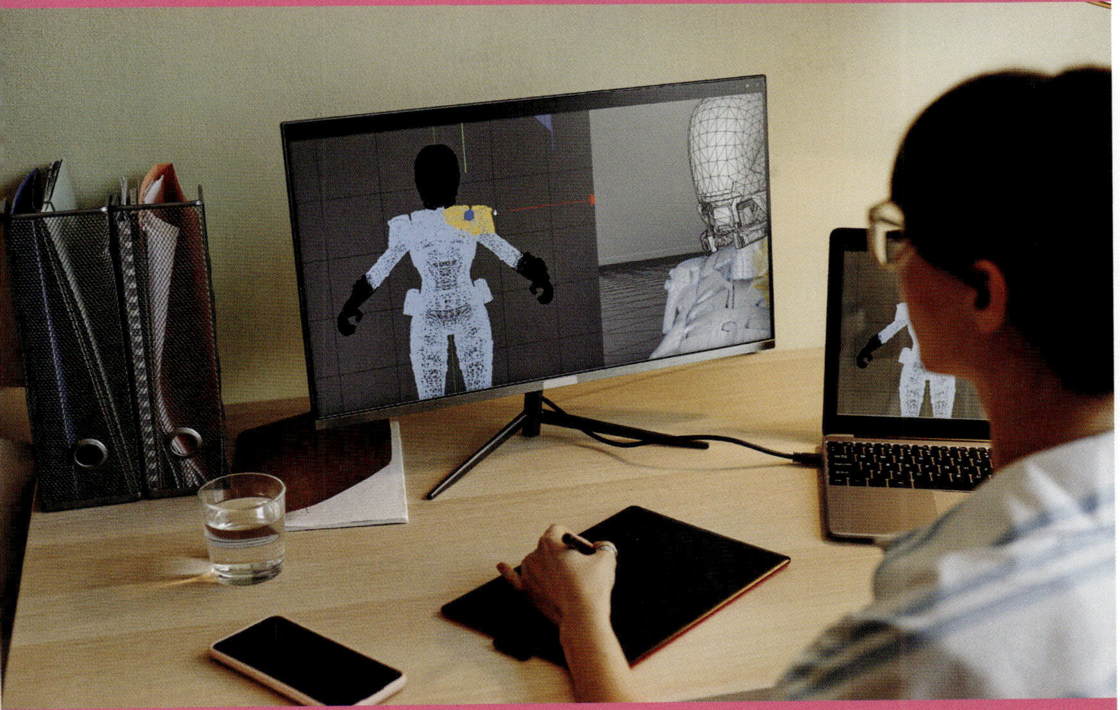

## Rigging

To make characters appear lifelike, computer animators sometimes use a process called rigging. It starts with the creation of a skeleton-like 3D model of a character. Animators can then move the model the way the character must move. By observing this movement and basing their work on it, they can make the animation look as realistic as possible.

# Chapter Five

# Breaking into Animation

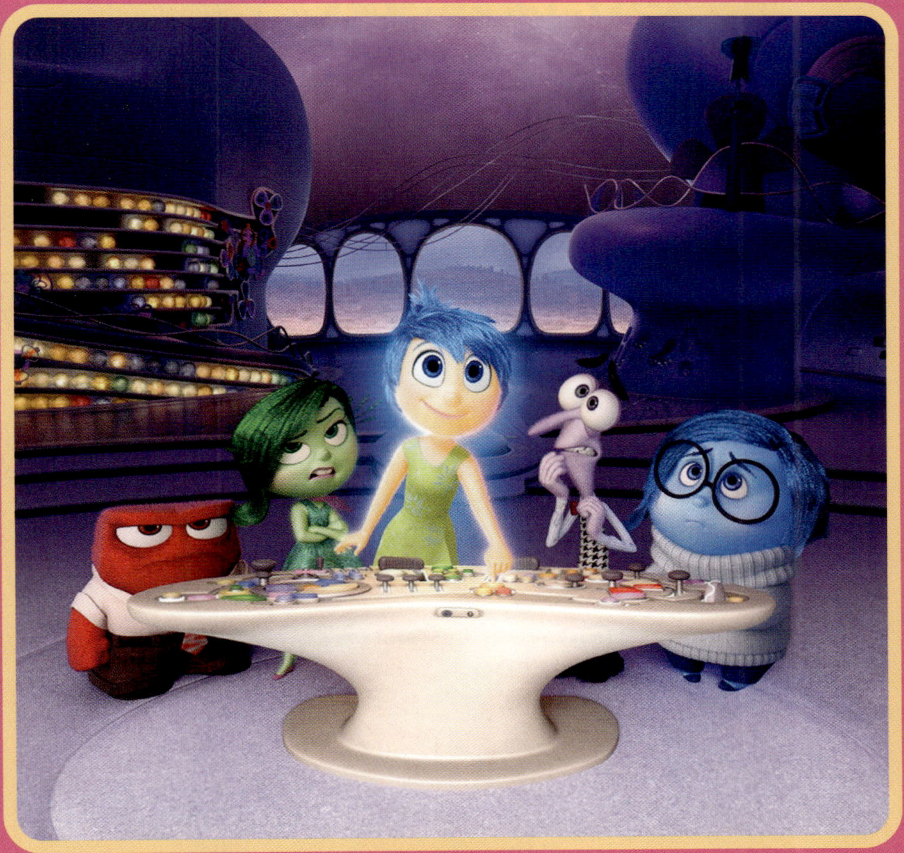

The best animators possess a true passion for art. But to be successful in this field, animators must know how to turn their talent into the practical skills that animation studios need. There are many things that artists can do to increase their chances of success.

# CHAPTER FIVE

Each type of animation requires different skill sets. From modeling and drawing to computer graphics, most animators have a **specialty**. This is often directly linked to an animator's greatest talent, but artists can also develop minor talents into valuable skills through education and practice.

One way to explore different skill sets is by attending an animation camp. Camps are offered by many colleges and art schools. They give students a chance to explore different forms of animation and to start developing skills.

Every animator needs a **portfolio**. From college admissions departments to animation studios, artists must show their work to many people to move forward in this career. There are several free websites where artists can display their portfolios. They can even upload examples to YouTube.

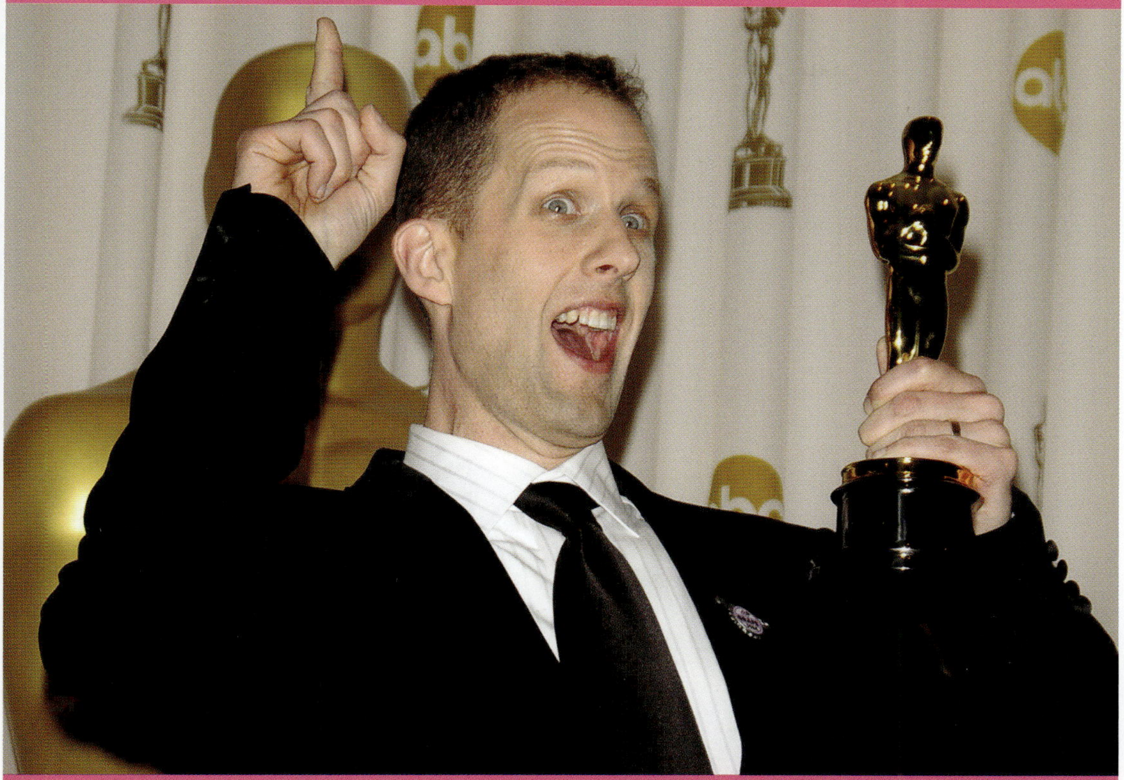

# Practice Makes Perfect

Even the best animators need practice to perfect their craft. Oscar-winning Pixar animator Pete Docter started out by making animated films to entertain friends. "Most of my stuff was bad, but I had fun, and I tried everything I knew to get better."

# CHAPTER FIVE

A great way to get started in animation is through an internship. Many studios have these programs in which young animators work side-by-side with more experienced artists. Some internships require college degrees. Others are specifically for college students.

To get an animation internship, an artist also needs a **demo reel**. This should be saved in the most current animation software. Animators hoping to snag an internship might also consider entering their work in animation competitions. Even small awards can help show a studio how talented an up-and-coming artist is.

# Breaking into Animation

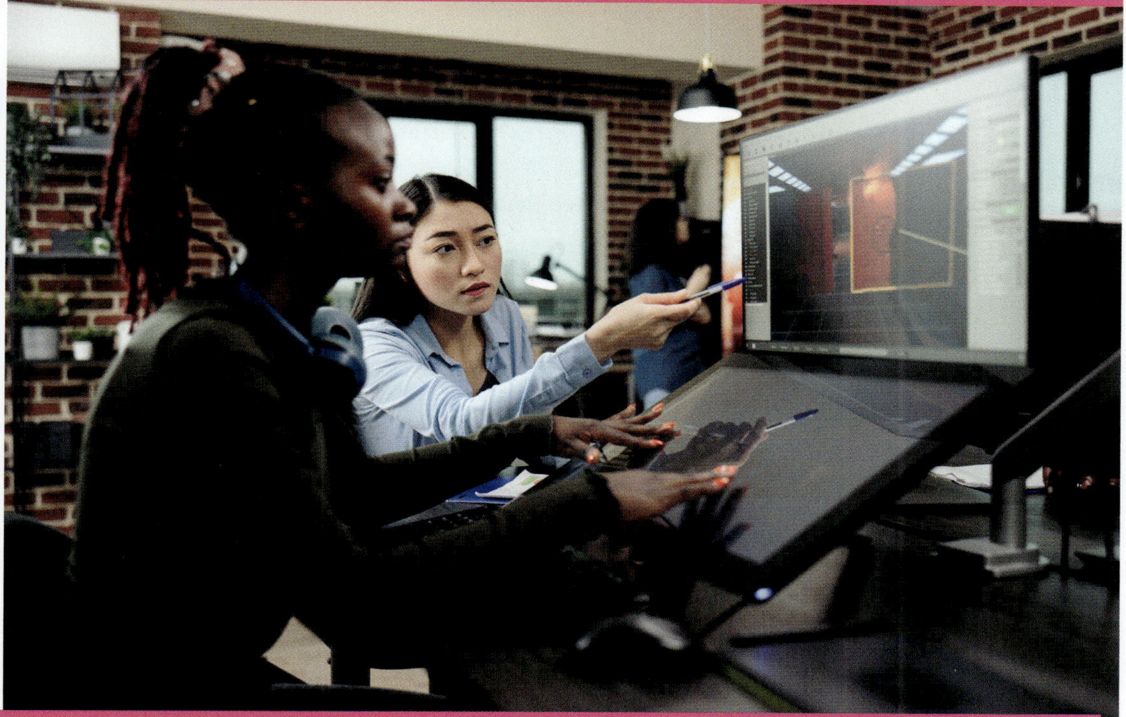

An internship can help budding animators grow their skills.

New animators may also consider joining an animation club. This type of group gives animators an opportunity to meet other people interested in animation. Club members can get feedback on their work and sometimes make connections with people in the industry.

Like internships, **apprenticeships** are another way to break into animation. These programs are often open to recent college graduates or artists with a few years of experience in animation. Apprenticeships can work well for both the animator and the studio. The apprentice gets on-the-job training and the possibility of a position with the company in the future. And the studio often gets a valuable animator who has been trained for its specific needs.

# Breaking into Animation

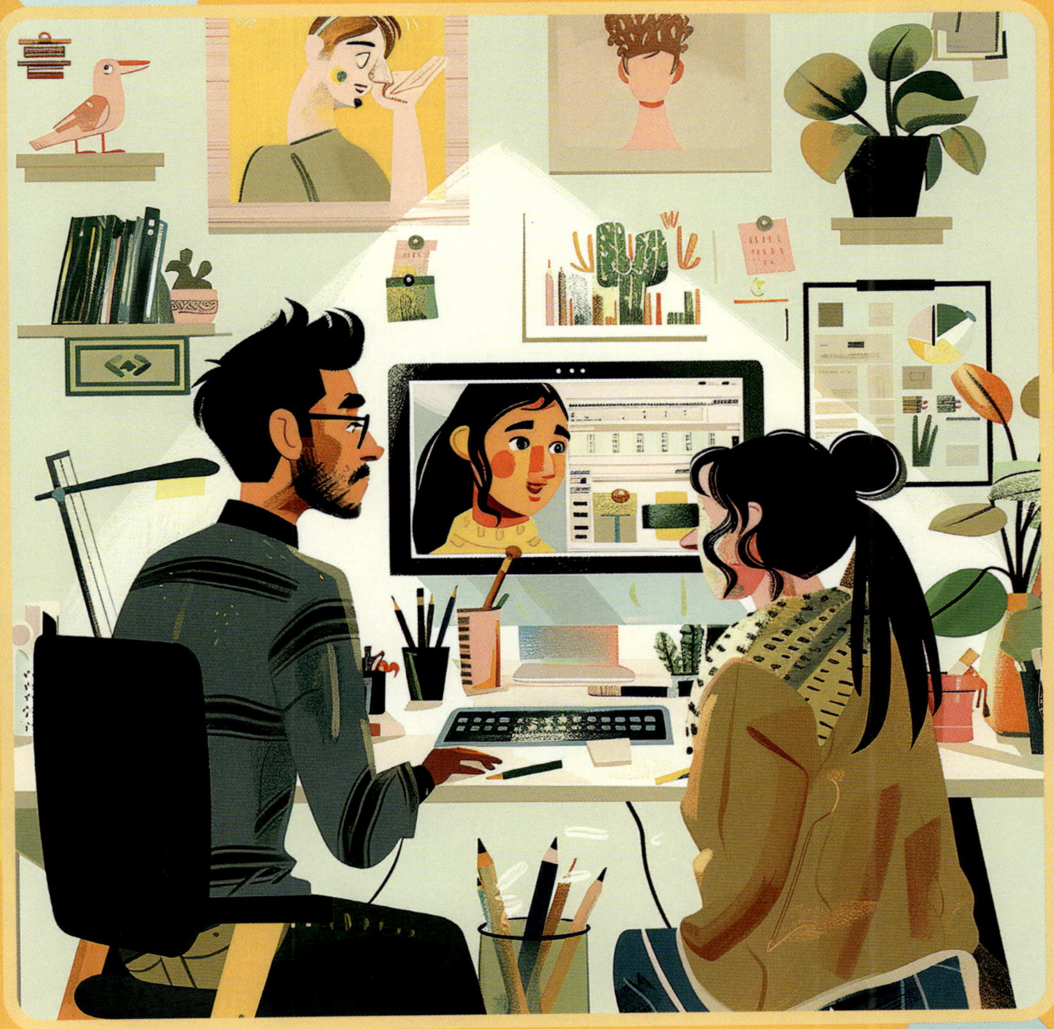

Being an apprentice can lead to a career with an animation studio.

# CHAPTER FIVE

In 2022, Disney brought back its hand-drawn animation apprenticeships after more than ten years. The apprentices worked on a short film, *Once Upon a Studio*, which revisited legendary Disney characters. In an interview on Disney's website, apprentice Austin Traylor said, "It's really inspiring to go online and see people chatting about *Once Upon a Studio*, saying, 'Maybe someday I could pursue traditional hand-drawn animation at Disney.'"

Animation is a fun and rewarding career. It takes a lot of time and effort. But for someone with the passion for bringing images to life, the hard work may be more than worth it. As Walt Disney once said, "All our dreams can come true, if we have the courage to pursue them."

# Breaking into Animation

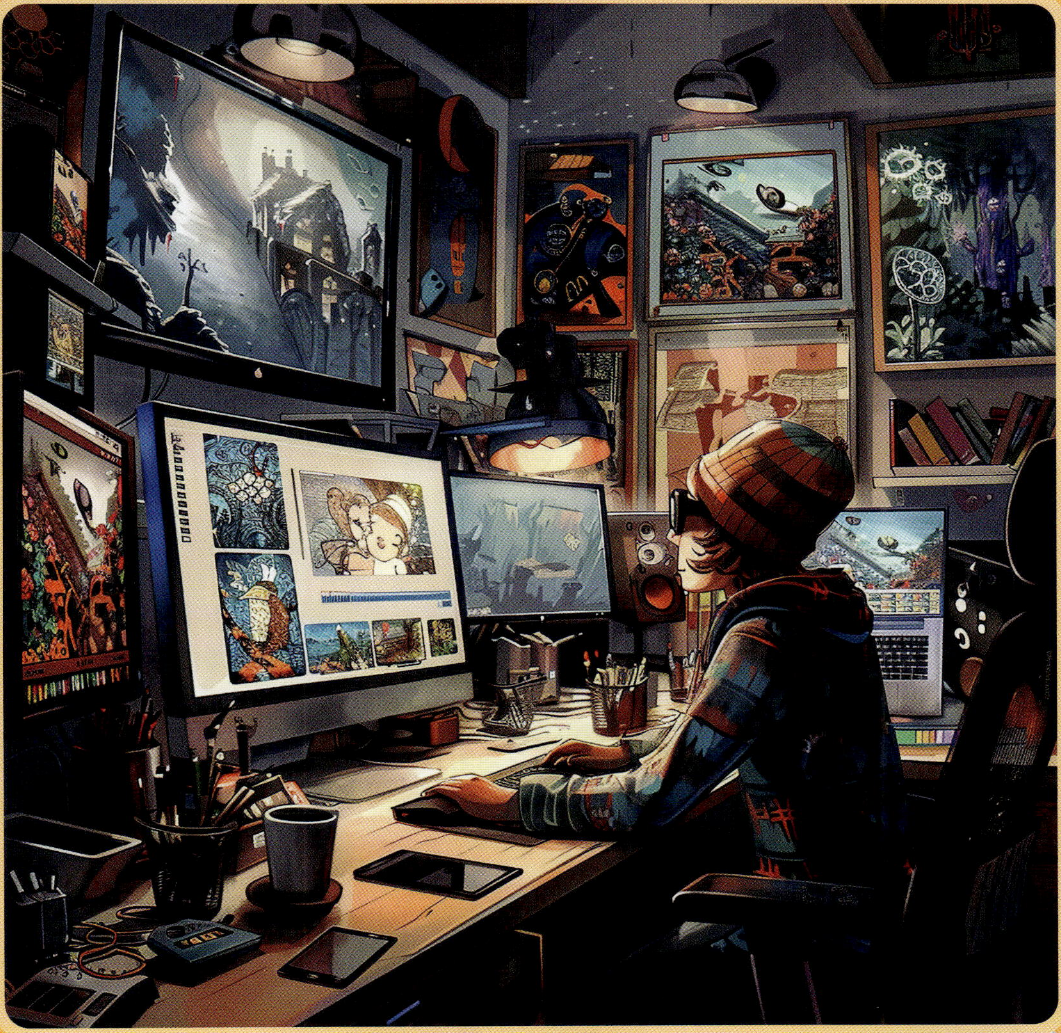

As an animator, the only limit is the artist's imagination.

# Glossary

**animated**
Made in the form of a cartoon

**apprenticeships**
Jobs given to people to learn a skill or trade

**consistency**
The ability to produce similar results repeatedly

**demo reel**
A short video presentation that showcases an individual's best work in film or television

**forensic**
Relating to scientific knowledge used for solving crimes

**internship**
A job given to a student for the purpose of gaining skills and experience

**nominated**
Named as a candidate for an award or honor

**portfolio**
A collection of an artist's best work

**specialty**
An area of exceptional skill or training

**succession**
A series of things that appear in a specific order

**transparent**
Easily seen through

# Ready, Set, Animate!

**Test your new knowledge of animation by answering the following questions.**

1. **When creating a flipbook, what gives the image its animated effect?**
   - **A.** Rapid changes
   - **B.** Gradual changes
   - **C.** No changes
2. **What was Walt Disney's first full-length film?**
   - **A.** *Beauty and the Beast*
   - **B.** *Toy Story*
   - **C.** *Snow White and the Seven Dwarfs*
3. **In stop motion animation, an object is:**
   - **A.** Photographed
   - **B.** Drawn by hand
   - **C.** Created by a computer
4. **Every animator needs a/an:**
   - **A.** College degree
   - **B.** Internship at a major studio
   - **C.** Portfolio

Answers: B, C, A, C

# Find Out More

## IN PRINT

Helt, Julianna. *A Career in Cartooning*. Mitchell Lane Publishers, 2026.

Levy, David B. *Your Career in Animation*. Allworth Press, 2021.

Roggio, Sarah. *Anime and Manga Artists*. ReferencePoint Press, 2024.

## ON THE INTERNET

**"Animation Courses and Certifications," *Class Central*, n.d.**
www.classcentral.com/subject/animation

**"What Does a Teenage Animator Do?" *Jobs for Teens HQ*, n.d.**
https://jobsforteenshq.com/how-to-become-a-teenage-animator

**"The Best Animation Summer Programs for High School Students," *College Gazette*, February 3, 2023.**
https://collegegazette.com/best-animation-summer-programs-for-high-school-students

# Index



## About the Author

**Kerry Kelaher Fredeen grew up in New Jersey watching Saturday morning cartoons and has loved animation ever since. She now lives in Hollywood, California, where she has written several books for young readers. When she's not busy writing, she works at a Southern California library.**